2020 VISION

DUMP TRUMP

ROGER H. HULL

All Rights Reserved

Copyright (c) 2019

Cover by Cathy Hull

Liz—
I hope both you
and this country will
soon be cured.

Rgh

A LESSON FROM THE PAST

"First they came for the socialists, and I did not speak out—because I was not a socialist.
Then they came for the trade unionists, and I did not speak out—because I was not a trade unionist.

Then they came for the Jews, and I did not speak out—because I was not a Jew.

Then they came for me—and there was no one left to speak for me."

Martin Niemöller, 1946

SUMMING IT ALL UP

It is foolish (and arrogant) for anyone to try to reduce serious problems to a sound-bite. Yet, paradoxically, Democrats need to do so. Even with an historically unpopular president, neither position papers nor long-winded responses will cut it in 2020.

In watching the Democratic primary process, it is obvious, if Democrats want to make Donald Trump a one-term president and recapture the Senate, they also need to jettison the circular-firing squad approach in which they are engaged. Doing anything else will give Trump a wounded opponent and alienate the other candidates' supporters.

Much as everything the fake president says and does is despicable (anyone who "wins" with Russian help and suppressed votes is, by definition, a fake president, even if duly elected), Trump does one thing very well: He hammers his message, however inaccurate and phony it might be, again and again. In 2020, his Democratic opponent needs to find a brief, clear, and convincing message and repeatedly drive it home, too.

Why? So voters can understand where the candidate stands. After all, the overwhelming majority of Americans have neither the time nor the inclination to delve into the minutiae of the issues the United States faces today.

We are at a pivotal moment in our history. If we are to restore civility, decency, fairness, morality, and the rule of law to the United States, if we are to become again a beacon of freedom for the world, we need to have Democrats seize the moment—and the Presidency and Senate. And to do so, a message that resonates with a majority of voters on a range of issues is essential.

For starters, Democrats might try crafting messages around the comments below to address the issues of 2020, comments that will be of appeal beyond the Democratic base. (For those interested in some background on each of the issues raised, it follows this summary.)

BIGOTRY— Remember that words matter, and that, all too often, racist words quickly turn into racist actions.

CORRUPTION—Pass legislation making self-dealing by a president illegal and requiring all presidential candidates to release their tax returns.

HEALTH CARE—Provide greater funding for Obamacare and continued protection for pre-existing conditions; and retain a role for private insurance as do all other countries that have universal health care coverage.

PRESCRIPTION DRUGS—Allow the government to negotiate drug prices and hold opioid manufacturers accountable.

IMMIGRATION—Secure the border; implement the 2013 Gang of 8 compromise; develop a "Marshall Plan" for El Salvador, Guatemala, and Honduras; and provide humanitarian assistance, as necessary, to illegal immigrants to maintain our core values.

REPARATIONS—Should not be an election issue and a particular group should not be singled out.

GUN CONTROL—Adopt red flag laws; pass extensive background check legislation; ban assault weapons and provide for voluntary buyback of those guns; and limit the size of magazine clips.

CLIMATE CHANGE—Acknowledge science reality; return to the Paris Climate Agreement; and embrace an incremental approach to a Green New Deal by setting up demonstration plants at the site of shuttered mines to develop public support from those in economically-affected areas.

TAXES—Recognize taxes should be fair and progressive, so we have the resources to tackle serious problems and, at the same time, begin to tackle the widening gap between the wealthy and the rest of the country.

INFRASTRUCTURE—Find ways to increase revenue to address the problem of the United States falling back to an almost developing country status.

NATIONAL DEBT—Grow the debt only if the Gross Domestic Product increases to avoid mortgaging our children's future.

TARIFFS—Avoid them, since they only work for "infant" industries, and they make consumers pay more for products.

STUDENT DEBT—Institute a national service plan to provide, in exchange for public service, college or trade school education, rather than make education "free."

FOREIGN POLICY—Abandon the concept of regime change, and rebuild frayed alliances to have partnerships in place to address mutually difficult geopolitical challenges.

MILITARY—Continue our role as policeman of the world so long as any action is taken with the participation of our allies and with Congressional oversight and adherence to constitutional principles; and help veterans with health, homelessness, and unemployment issues.

JUDICIAL SYSTEM—Recognize the need to win elections to prevent the courts from becoming more conservative, but reject packing the Supreme Court as an answer for past election failures.

CRIMINAL JUSTICE REFORM—Realize the First Step Act is a first step (not the last one) to reduce the prison population, with the elimination of mandatory minimum sentences part of the solution to this problem.

A WOMAN'S RIGHT TO CHOOSE—Insure Roe v. Wade remains the law of the land, but respect those who hold a different opinion.

VOTING RIGHTS—End voter suppression by eliminating ID laws, the closing of polling stations, and the purging of names from voter rolls to insure this basic right is retained.

CAMPAIGN FINANCING—Seek to overturn <u>Citizen's United</u> and implement campaign finance limits that can withstand legal challenges.

THE ECONOMY—Realize that, despite a weak recovery, we have had 121 months of sustained growth, as well as a soaring stock market, with gains, percentage-wise, twice as great under Obama than Trump (historically, stock market gains have been far stronger under Democrats than Republicans).

ENERGY—Keep pressure on Republicans nationally to develop alternatives to fossil fuels and work with Democratic governors and legislatures to implement those alternatives.

DEREGULATION—Unwind as soon as possible Trump's environmental, education, and banking rollbacks to protect America and Americans.

MINIMUM WAGE—Recognize one size does not fit all, increase the minimum wage regionally, and index it to inflation.

EQUAL PAY FOR WOMEN—Of course

A LITTLE BACKGROUND

In 2020, those Americans who want a more civil, decent, fairer, and moral country that embraces the rule of law have a two-fold challenge: driving Donald J. Trump from the White House, which is their primary focus, and recapturing the Senate, which too few of them recognize is essential. One without the other simply will not work.

A century before this nation was fractured by the Vietnam War, we endured a far more cataclysmic split in the United States—the Civil War. In that conflict, roughly 620,000 Americans lost their lives and hundreds of thousands of others were maimed.

We have come a long way from that dismal point in our history. Yet the anger on both sides of the divide over Donald Trump is obvious.

Regardless of one's views, we should not demonize those who feel and think differently from us. For Trump and his allies to label everyone opposing him and his policies a socialist is ridiculous. So, too, is calling all of the president's supporters racists and "deplorable."

Much has changed from the 1940s and 1950s and even the 1970s, when racists were at home in the Democratic Party (remember George Wallace?). Today, they have migrated to the Republican Party.

But the racist label clearly does not apply to all Trump supporters. Neither does misogynist or homophobe or xenophobe, although those labels can certainly be attached to some of Trump's voters.

Others of Trump's supporters in 2016 were simply Republicans. Life-long members of the party, they could not support a Democrat, much less a Clinton.

In addition to those members of Trump's base, some of his support came from those whose focus was on gaining more wealth. Rather than recognizing that, in the long run, neither they nor anyone else wins when the gap between rich and poor continues to widen, they voted for promises of tax breaks and deregulation.

Importantly, though, some of Trump's support came from factory workers, who voted for Obama in 2008 and 2012, but who had not seen a rise in pay for a decade or two and who cast their ballots for Trump in 2016. What label would best apply to them? How about frustrated?

Reaching those who are strong Trump supporters is probably impossible. Getting to those who were left behind by closed factories or outsourcing is a different matter. So, too, is getting to educated, suburban, Republican women.

What should a message be to reach those folks? For that matter, what should it be to those who are independents?

"Not Trump," despite many voices to the contrary, will not carry the day in 2020. While a recent survey showed 57% would never vote for Trump in 2020, those numbers—if accurate (and the polls in 2016 might well lead one to question their accuracy)—do not necessarily mean those opposed to Trump will vote for the Democratic candidate.

Instead, "Never Trumpers" might choose to vote for an independent candidate. Or they might do what many did in 2016—stay home and not vote.

For those strongly opposed to Trump and his policies, the Democratic primary process should be viewed with alarm and disgust. How can one not be alarmed and disgusted when Democratic presidential candidates pander to see which of them can lurch most to the left to appease the so-called Democratic base.

Democratic activists are fired up. If they, the young, and those who stayed home in 2016 went to the polls in 2020, Democrats can win. And, as political pundits have pointed out, white college graduates are increasingly progressive.

But how many of those white college graduates who are increasingly progressive live in the battleground states of Arizona, Florida, Michigan, Ohio, Pennsylvania, and Wisconsin? More importantly, do those on the hard left understand they are playing Russian roulette with several bullets in the gun's chamber, pointing that gun at our collective heads, and putting the American experiment at risk?

Having the courage of one's convictions is important. Yet striving for principles that, in this divisive climate, are unattainable makes absolutely no political sense.

A presidential campaign is a good place to put forth a new idea or two. It is not a place for floating "principles" that, in effect, compromise what should be Democrats' principal goals in 2020—driving Trump from the White House and recapturing the Senate.

Talking about making illegal entry into the United States a civil (not criminal) violation, the elimination of private insurance, and health care for those crossing into the country illegally is political suicide. Aside from the fact that none of these issues will fly politically in a divided Congress, the reality is the issues will be liabilities in a presidential campaign, at least in battleground states.

For that matter, talk of eliminating the Electoral College, packing the Supreme Court, and reparations for African-Americans are not ideas that should be part of the presidential debate. So far as the general election is concerned, they are political losers.

It is almost as if the Trump campaign has placed political operatives in the Democratic Party. How else to explain advancing far-reaching, divisive ideas that have no place on the campaign trail, unless the goal is to drive voters opposed to Trump to him or, more likely, to have them stay home in 2020?

The old refrain is capture the nomination, then tack to the center. However, those advocating "progressive" positions have no interest in moving to the center after securing the nomination. Besides, in a day of instant electronic communications, it is hard to see how an image of, for instance, hands raised during a Democratic debate in response to a question about who would eliminate private insurance is a formula for political success.

At least it is not a formula for political success in a country that has, over the years, been moving to the right. A few quick numbers underscore this reality.

In 1964, conservative Republican Barry Goldwater got electorally swamped by Lyndon Johnson (486-52). By 1972, though, when Democrats nominated liberal George McGovern, the results were reversed, and McGovern won only one state and the District of Columbia and lost electorally 520-17. And in 1980 Ronald Reagan beat Jimmy Carter electorally 489-49, and in 1984, he politically slaughtered Walter Mondale by 525-13.

With the country moving inexorably to the right, will going left, especially hard left, work in 2020? Doubtful—even with an historically unpopular president.

Besides, Democrats seem to be oblivious to the fact they are not the largest political grouping in the country. Neither are Republicans. That distinction belongs to independents.

In a Gallop 2019 survey, 27% of Americans identified themselves as Republicans, and 29% called themselves Democrats. But 40% of those surveyed said they were independents.

How many of those who call themselves independents are interested in eliminating private health insurance or, in effect, opening our borders or giving illegal entrants to this country better health care than 35 million Americans have? Not many.

Democrats need to ask themselves, for the sake of all of us, a simple question: What is their goal? Is it to speak to issues that are important to some and anathema to others or to keep their eyes on the real prizes—winning back the White House and the Senate and returning this country to a land of civility, decency, and the rule of law.

To recapture 1600 Pennsylvania Avenue and the Senate, Democrats need to try to get back some of those who voted for Barack Obama in 2008 and 2012, but who then voted for Donald Trump in 2016. More importantly, they need to get back some of the 4.4 million who voted for Obama in 2012 but did not vote in 2016.

Even if Trump is defeated and the House of Representatives is retained in Democratic hands, change will not come. So long as the Senate remains in Republican hands, which means Mitch McConnell's hands, little can be accomplished legislatively.

We need to remember, as many Democrats and independents know, it was McConnell who single-handedly refused to give Merrick Garland a vote on his nomination to the open Supreme Court seat following the death of Antonin Scalia. And we all know what happened next—and what may well happen in the future if McConnell remains the Senate Majority leader.

The allure of the presidency is intoxicating. While being a governor or senator should be of great appeal, it clearly is less appealing than working at 1600 Pennsylvania Avenue for a number of those in the Democratic pubic spotlight.

Democrats like Stacy Abrams, Steve Bullock, and Beto O'Rourke should wipe the presidential fairy dust from their eyes and recognize that, were Democrats to capture Senate seats in Georgia, Montana, and Texas through their efforts, we would be well on our way to being a far better country, even if (God forbid) the current occupant of the White House is reelected. (John Hickenlooper recently dropped out of the presidential sweepstakes and is now running for the Senate from Colorado; other strong Democratic senatorial candidates should follow suit.)

Trump cannot win reelection without Democratic help. So far, Democrats are giving him plenty of help.

All-too-often, the perfect is the enemy of the good. For Democrats to put forth politically unattainable ideas, engage in internecine warfare, damage viable candidates for the basest of political reasons, and require a form of political purity is insane. We as a nation cannot afford that insanity, not at this critical point in our political history.

It is important for Democrats to air their ideas. However, they should air politically viable ideas that can be used effectively both in a primary and a general election. And Democrats should learn to see the impact of their actions on people within and, importantly, outside the Democratic Party.

Fighting over ideas, politically practical ideas, is also important. Those fights will only strengthen the Democratic standard-bearer in the 2020 general election with Trump. By the same token, forming a circular firing squad as the Democrats seem now to be engaged in will critically wound, if not kill, the Democratic nominee.

Finding an "aha" moment may score points during a Democratic primary debate (one need look no further than Kamala Harris' attack of Joe Biden on busing), but it may well have long-lasting negative results for the ultimate Democratic nominee. Remember 2016?

As a result of the games played by the Democratic National Committee and its Chair Debbie Wasserman Schultz, Bernie Sanders was not given a fair shake in his battle with Hillary Clinton. How many of his voters stayed home in an election where an aggregate of 77,000 votes were the margin of victory in Michigan, Pennsylvania, and Wisconsin?

Getting the right messenger will, obviously, be key in 2020 if Democrats are to recapture the White House. It will also be key if they are to have any chance of winning control of the Senate and retaining control of the House because the wrong standard bearer will greatly lessen Democratic senatorial candidates' chances in several states.

The message will also be key. Right now Democrats do not have one, other than "we are not Trump." Democrats need a message—and they need it now!

At this point, there is only one person, who is a messenger and who has a message—Congresswoman Alexandria-Ocasio Cortez. She is smart, and she is the only person on the political scene who can articulate her beliefs briefly and incredibly well. Yet, paradoxically, Ocasio-Cortez is also incredibly dangerous politically because her message will not play (positively) in battleground states.

Ocasio-Cortez wants to pull the Democratic Party to the left; and she has said she wants to have progressive candidates challenge elected Democrats who do not share her beliefs. While she has every right to those beliefs, the fact remains the Democrats would not have won control of the House of Representatives in 2018 if they had followed her platform—Medicare for All, canceling of all student debt, fully funded (free) public colleges and universities, a universal jobs guarantee with a $15 minimum wage pegged to inflation, and housing as a right.

For every Ocasio-Cortez, for every Congresswoman-colleague of hers like Ilhan Oman, Ayanna Pressley, and Rashida Tlaib (the "Squad," as Trump pejoratively calls them), there were seven moderate Democrats who beat sitting Republican Congressmen in 2018. Simply stated, moderates, not progressives, were the reason Democrats won control of the House of Representatives during the last Congressional elections.

In 2020, as in 2016, Democrats will certainly win in the nation's cities; they need to win in the suburbs, though, to gain control in Washington. For them to do so, they will need the suburban Republican women of Detroit, Miami, Milwaukee, Philadelphia, Phoenix, Northern Virginia, and the cities of Ohio.

A "Democratic Socialist," as members of the Squad refer to themselves, will not bring suburban Republican women to the Democrats. While they might not vote for Trump in 2020, those women will probably stay home—and we, as a nation, cannot afford to have them do so.

Elections obviously have consequences. From the composition of the Supreme Court to key legislation, a range of issues of import to Democrats and independents are at risk if Democrats do not effectively coalesce around a candidate with appeal beyond an active Democratic base.

While Democrats seem adept at fighting among themselves, Republicans are unified. Having abandoned their longstanding beliefs and made their Faustian bargain with the devil, they want simply to retain power and win at all costs.

If the Democrats win the 2020 elections, they can begin a discussion of other legislative ideas. Now, though, is not the time for focusing on pie-in-the-sky beliefs, catering solely on the Democrats' progressive base, or for attacks on those who might be the last, best hope for returning this country to civility, morality, and the rule of law.

Conversely, now is the time to undo the mistakes of 2016, so we can return to fairness and decency in the United States. And now is the time to recognize the obvious: The 2020 election will turn on convincing independents to support a Democratic nominee for President and Democratic nominees for the Senate, so we can all wake up from our national nightmare.

ISSUES
FACTS
RECOMMENDATIONS

Let's be clear, crystal clear. While tens of millions of people in the United States feel Donald J. Trump is a racist, who is, at best, ignorant of this country's history and traditions, millions of others feel he truly does represent their interests and values.

It is tempting to argue that, if one supports someone who is a racist, one is a racist oneself. Perhaps. It is better, though, to discard labels and deal with reality, and the reality is, for Trump supporters, Trump has delivered.

No, Trump hasn't built his wall, despite his claims to the contrary, and Mexico certainly has not paid for any portion of it. But the 5-4 Supreme Court decision allowing him to take funds earmarked for the military for wall construction helps the President going into the 2020 election cycle to make the argument he is building the wall.

Trump has, though, slashed regulations everywhere; he has benefitted from the economic turnaround begun by Barack Obama (which Trump would never acknowledge and which his tariffs threaten to undermine); he has built up the military; and he has populated the judiciary with hard-right appointments. To his base, therefore, he has delivered (although it is clear any Republican would have done the same thing, without the hateful, harmful rhetoric).

Still, there are two operative questions posed by past Republican presidential candidates that voters will have to answer in 2020: i) "Are you better off today than you were four years ago" (Ronald Reagan, 1980); and ii) "What do you have to lose" (a question Trump directed to African-Americans in 2016)?

So what is the approach Democrats should take in 2020? In particular, what should their approach be to independents on the many issues that will be before voters?

In (briefly and incompletely) examining the issues, one thing is patently obvious—not all issues are created equal. While a particular issue might well resonate with some voters, other issues will be of greater import to larger groups of voters.

We also need to be cognizant of the fact that issues have greater or lesser appeal in different sections of the country. Most political pundits agree the Democratic nominee will win the popular vote by racking up votes in the nation's largest cities.

But will a Democratic presidential candidate be able to garner the requisite 270 electoral votes in the Electoral College. And will that nominee make it more or less likely the Democrats can recapture the Senate? In the final analysis, the answers to these questions are all that matter

BIGOTRY

At this point, one should not be arguing about whether or not the President is a racist, misogynist, homophobe, or xenophobe. If it looks like a duck, quacks like a duck, and waddles like a duck, it is a duck.

The present occupant of 1600 Pennsylvania Avenue may claim he "does not have a prejudiced bone in his body." However, his words paint a very different picture.

Besides whether Trump actually believes the hateful gibberish he spews or mouths his words for political purposes is irrelevant. Either way, he is making it respectable for others to follow his lead and turn the clock back to an ugly time in American history.

The recent shooting spree in El Paso, where Mexican-Americans were targeted, is an obvious example of how words matter. From the postings of Trump's words on the killer's electronic accounts, we have learned the shooter, a white supremacist, expressed strong support for Trump and KKK leader David Duke, who apparently took to heart Trump's words about Mexicans being "rapists and murders."

Throughout history there have been many cases of political leaders using groups of people for purposes of dividing a population. American presidents have not been immune to this type of effort; however, never before Trump has a president so blatantly sought to divide Americans and use that division to further his political ends.

We have all been taught the end does not justify the means. Apparently, Trump never learned that lesson. For him, everything is transactional; for him, there are only winners and losers. So, in his mind, one needs to win at all costs.

But what is the price people like Trump pay for this misguided approach? Some might argue, not much. After all, he is president, and those that criticize him are not.

Others, though, feel very differently. For them, it matters how one does something because the end, in fact, does not justify the means.

For a nation, of course, how one does something matters greatly. Not only is our stature in the world negatively impacted by the words and actions of this president, but so, too, is the very soul of this land.
Civility matters. Morality matters. How one says and does things matter.

And yet, despite our highly charged political climate, it is fair to ask whether a president who has conducted himself as Trump has is disqualified to lead this nation. In the view of many, he never was qualified, and his words disqualify him for a second term.

But to 40% of the populace, a percentage that appears to be rock-solid, Trump is qualified. In their mind, he clearly warrants reelection.

To prevent his reelection, it will not be enough to speak of his lack of civility and morality. Still, it is absolutely essential to remind voters that we are indeed better, individually and as a country, than Donald J. Trump portrays us to the rest of the world.

Words matter, and they always will. And when those words are expressed by the President of the United States, they matter all the more.

After all, if crying "fire in a crowded theater" is not protected speech because of the panic that will ensue (as Oliver Wendell Holmes opined in 1919 in Schenk v. United States), why should the president of the United States be able to use inflammatory words which, in Holmes' words, present a "clear and present danger"? He clearly should not.

The clear and present danger of Trump extends beyond our shores, of course. Commenting on African nations on the subject of immigration, Trump asked why America would want immigrants from "all these shithole countries," and, he added, the United States should have more people from places like Norway.

And Trump's rant about the Squad (which will undoubtedly be part of his 2020 campaign "message") also harms the United States worldwide. In referring to the four Congresswomen, Trump tweeted "why don't they go back and help fix the totally broken and crime infested places from which they came?" (Of course, since three of the four women were born in the United States, the tweet, in effect, slams the United States and Trump's administration.)

Inflammatory? Yes. Helpful to the United States? Clearly not.

CORRUPTION

During his campaign run, one of Trump's rallying cries was "drain the swamp." Rather than doing so, he has widened and deepened it and caused it to reek. In effect, the President has turned the swamp into a cesspool.

For a very long time, the United States has had its share of corruption. However, we have never witnessed corruption emanating from the Oval Office itself.

Historical examples of corruption abound. Some were big, some small. Among the former: the gold speculation ring involving Ulysses Grant's cabinet, and Warren Harding's Teapot Dome scandal (Harding's Secretary of the Interior went to jail for accepting bribes over the leasing of oil reserves, resulting in Congress passing legislation giving it subpoena power over the tax records of American citizens, legislation that clearly applies to Trump himself).

On the other end of the spectrum, there is Sherman Adams, Dwight D. Eisenhower's chief of staff. He lost his position for accepting a vicuna coat and an antique rug. How far we have fallen!

But history also provides us with positive examples. Harry Truman stands out.

Unlike many of those who preceded and succeeded him, Truman had limited resources. Even after he left office and his income fell from his $100,000 presidential salary to roughly $15,000 (his military pension, since, until 1958, presidents did not receive a pension from the government), Truman "could never lend (him)self to any transaction, however respectable, that would commercialize on the prestige and dignity of the office of the presidency."

Yes, some former presidents have garnered great wealth after their presidency. Book deals and speaking fees are generally the reason for that wealth (Truman also sold his memoirs, the proceeds of which enabled his annual income to return to the level he had enjoyed in the White House).

As for the present occupant of the White House, he has suggested foreign officials stay at his Washington hotel, a violation of the Emoluments Clause of the Constitution. He also refused, as his predecessors had, to place his assets in a qualified blind trust, defined as a trust in which the trustee has no relation to the government official establishing the trust; instead, Trump made his sons, Don Jr. and Eric, his trustees.
Trump has also financially benefitted from taxpayers paying for golf cart rentals for Secret Service members at his clubs (Trump, who blasted

Obama for playing golf and claimed he would be too busy to play golf himself because he would be working fulltime for the American people, has played roughly triple the amount of golf Obama did during a comparable period). In addition, he has sold properties to Russians during his presidency, rented space to foreign entities in Trump Tower, and engaged in ongoing self-dealing.

Continuing down the money trail: At a G-7 meeting, Trump shamelessly suggested a meeting of the G-7 be held at his Doral golf club; his vice president went to a meeting in Dublin, Ireland (on the East coast of the island), but his hotel was a Trump property on the West coast; his Attorney General decided to host a holiday party at Trump's Washington hotel; and Trump had a deal with the Glasgow airport to send flight crews to his Turnberry resort in Ireland when they overnighted (to date, 40 United States Air Force crews have overnighted at Turnberry).

To really follow the money, though, one needs to see Trump's tax returns. Yet, despite his claim throughout the 2016 campaign that he would release them but for the fact he was under IRS audit (there was never any proof Trump was under audit, and there is no prohibition about the release of tax returns while a person is under audit), those tax returns have never been released. So, no one knows from whom Trump has received loans and to whom he is indebted.

Hardly a pretty or an ethical way of doing things. So long as Trump occupies 1600 Pennsylvania Avenue and the Republican Party continues to engage in its Faustian bargain with him, though, nothing will change.

When things do change, it is imperative for a Democratically-controlled Congress and a Democratic president to make the type of activities we have been exposed to since 2016 illegal and to require every presidential candidate to release past tax returns. The presidency should not be a cash cow for the White House occupant.

HEALTH CARE

Ever since James Carville said "it's the economy, stupid," it has been the common wisdom that jobs are the key to victory for any presidential candidate. Maybe. And, with the president having the benefit of 2% economic growth (not the 4%, 5%, or 6% he was predicting, but growth, nevertheless), falling interest rates, full employment, and a rising stock market in which more than half of Americans are invested, Trump would appear to have an obvious built-in advantage in his reelection bid.

Maybe not, though, in 2020. For many Americans, the cost of rising health care is of great concern. While the economy may be doing well, they are not, even though they may be experiencing a slight uptick in pay. Health care costs are often the reason.

Those costs, of course, only apply to those who have health care. In 32 of 33 developed countries, there is universal health care. The United States is the exception.

Health care, as many Democratic candidates have stated, should be a right, not a privilege. The question, of course, is how to provide for that right. In a very real sense, we already have universal health care, when the emergency room is factored in. Unfortunately, for a large number of Americans, that is how they receive their care.

Medicare for All sounds right to many Democratic presidential candidates—and to most Americans. Is it? Three issues quickly come to mind: cost, private insurance, and the impact on hospitals in general and rural hospitals in particular.

Medicare certainly works well for those who are covered by it. Expanding it to cover everyone, though, has a huge price tag—roughly $33 trillion over 10 years.

To insert an additional $3.3 trillion a year into the federal budget is hardly a trivial matter. In fact, the amount represents roughly five times what we spend annually on the military and is almost the size of the $4 trillion 2018 budget.

Importantly, it is impossible to provide for universal coverage without tax increases, tax increases that will impact everyone. While it is true individuals would save significant dollars by not having to pay premiums or deductibles, it is equally true it will be next to impossible to explain to voters, in the midst of an election campaign, that the benefit will exceed the cost to them.

As for private insurance, candidates have (rightly) been beating up on insurance companies. Some of the candidates want to eliminate private insurance; others want to phase it out over a period of years; and still others want to retain it as an option for those who want to keep their private insurance.

For those who favor the elimination of private insurance and a pure single-payer system, they are, presumably knowingly, changing what Medicare presently covers. Since Medicare provides for 80% of the cost of (covered) procedures, the remaining 20% is the responsibility of the individual. Eliminating private insurance means the cost to taxpayers goes up, with the counter argument being the cost to the individual might well go down.

Arguing, too, that 150 million Americans should abandon their private insurance is a position that will not fly in many quarters. During contract negotiations, union representatives often fought to give members health care benefits, rather than salary increases.

Taking those benefits away and having everyone covered by Medicare will make for a difficult, if not impossible, political sale, since salary increases will have been "waived" for no corresponding benefit. (Medicare for All proponents argue, without any evidence to support their claim, employers will give employees pay increases to cover the benefit they won through negotiations and will now relinquish because they will no longer have to pay for health insurance.)

Surprisingly, no candidate has pointed out that every one—every one—of the 32 developed countries that provide for universal health coverage also has private insurance. Some countries require all citizens to have private insurance; others have private insurers who supplement what is covered by public insurance; and still others have private insurance that provides for faster service for procedures that are covered.

If one is going to argue we should do what the rest of the developed world does, we should do what those countries, in fact, do. We should retain a role for private insurance.

Another issue no one is discussing, either, is the delay in obtaining health care in developed countries with universal health care. Importantly, too, no one is mentioning health care is rationed in those countries, with procedures not being available to people of a specified age as a way of reducing cost.

And then there is the impact of Medicare for All on hospitals, particularly rural hospitals. Some of those hospitals are now closing; more will close tomorrow; and still more will close the day after tomorrow when, assuming the implementation of a Medicare for All system, the reduced payments Medicare makes to those hospitals will put added pressure on them.

So where does one go and what does one do? "Incrementalism."

While Medicare for All proponents derisively attacked those, like Joe Biden, who want to build on the Affordable Care Act (Obamacare) as "incrementalists" who lack a bold vision, those proponents need to look at the big picture. Viewed through a political lens and believing we need to protect the health rights of individuals, an incrementalist approach makes sense.

Providing greater funding for Obamacare, continuing to protect pre-existing conditions, and establishing a public option for those who want a Medicare for All-type program is a good first step. (We might also try to educate patients about having fewer tests, as a way to reduce health care costs.)

Will it work? Maybe, if it were to be implemented.

The irony is, having fought Trump and his acolytes over the repeal of Obamacare and having been saved by Senator John McCain's dramatic, early morning refusal to go along with his fellow

Republicans at the last minute, Democrats are actually now leading the charge to overturn it. But they are not alone.

A legal challenge to Obamacare will soon work its way to the Supreme Court. Since the Supreme Court affirmed the legality of the Affordable Care Act in a 5-4 decision, with Justice Roberts casting the decisive fifth vote and basing his vote on the government's taxing power, Obamacare's future is very much in doubt given the fact Congress eliminated the "tax" (penalty) on people who failed to sign up for coverage.

PRESCRIPTION DRUGS

The price of prescription drugs is something that every politician, from Trump to those who want to take his place in the Oval Office, constantly references. Not only are prices incredibly high in far too many instances, but they are almost inexplicable in all cases.

Recently, a dermatologist phoned a prescription into the pharmacy. When I went to pick it up, I was told it cost $1000, but I could get it for "only" $600 (a cream to be used once a day for 28 days). I said I would talk to my dermatologist.

Two hours later, she prescribed a drug for $100, then called to say the company would not accept Medicare. Finally, another carrier provided the cream for $60.

Does this type of policy make any sense? Not to me; not to most Americans.

Why aren't Americans and their political representatives doing something about the issue. Perhaps because no one seems to pay the sticker price.

Of course, there are egregious cases that quickly come to mind—epinephrine, which Mylan Pharmaceuticals has increased five-fold in a little more than a decade, and insulin, which has tripled in the past 15 years. And then there is Martin Shkreli's daraprim, a drug used to treat AIDS, that Shkreli increased 5000% (before he went to jail).

What can be done? Government intervention. (Not price controls, which have been shown not to work.) But the government certainly could flex its financial muscles.

In the past, drug prices were based on a business model that was a combination of development and operating costs, together with a return on the investment made. Not so today, when price is tied more to the perceived value of the drug based on longevity or quality of life, combined with maximizing investment returns.

This more recent formula can be stated simply: Price is based on what the industry feels it can get away with. And, since consumers do not pay the daunting "sticker price" because of various assistance programs, those prices are far higher than their value should dictate. In effect, while individual patients are not paying for those inflated drug prices, we all are doing so because whatever patient-assistance programs exist are factored into the price of the drug.

If drug prices are not being priced fairly, there needs to be a way to control those prices. Among those ways are taxes on corporate profits, compulsory licensing of drugs to other manufacturers, tying the price of drugs to the price of that drug in other countries, or refusing to cover overpriced drugs (as determined by a panel of independent experts) in government-sponsored programs (Medicare and Medicaid).

Another possibility is to use the government's potential bargaining power. By giving the government the power to negotiate price (which it presently does not have), the prices for drugs would, presumably, be reduced.

Hospitals, which are negatively impacted by escalating drug prices that have grown roughly 20% annually for the past three years, can also play a major role. Recently, Memorial Sloan Kettering refused to use a cancer drug, listed at $100,000/year, because the drug extended the patient's life by less than two months, but it cost twice as much as a competing, equally-effective drug. (The manufacturer of the cancer drug subsequently cut the price in half.)

Despite egregious examples of price-gauging (Mylan and Shkreli), and despite the impact of price increases to hospitals, prescription drug prices are only a part of the problem of health care costs. Of those costs, drug prices represent roughly 20%.

Aside from the cost issue, of course, there is the epidemic in America of opioid abuse and addiction. Addressing the misuse of these drugs through clinician awareness (how often does a patient seek opioid prescription renewals, for instance?) can serve to identify where patient problems exist. So, too, can preventing or stopping the nonmedical use of prescription drugs.

Holding opioid manufacturers legally responsible for their role in the crisis is part of the solution. Accountability by opioid manufacturers for failing to properly inform patients of the addictive nature of the drugs is another part. And education, of patients by doctors and by the drug manufacturers themselves, is also a part of the solution.

Certainly, financial settlements or trials involving opioid manufacturers will continue. Unfortunately, they will not solve the problem, but the accountability of drug companies in the crisis remains important. After all, accountability is always important.

IMMIGRATION

We all know Emma Lazarus's powerful message on the Statue of Liberty—"Give me your tired masses yearning to be free." Conveniently forgetting they themselves are immigrants (or descendants of immigrants), many in the Trump administration (and his followers) want to shut America's door in the face of today's immigrants. Or, unbelievably, they want proof immigrants can stand financially on their own two feet before being granted admission.

There is a difference, though, between welcoming those "yearning to be free" and allowing anyone/everyone into the United States. And that difference is crucial for a Democratic candidate's prospects in 2020, since being for open, unsecured borders may well help put Trump back in the White House.

For starters, Democrats should embrace the Senate's Gang of Eight proposal of 2013. The proposal, agreed to by four Democrats and four Republicans (Schumer (D-NY), McCain (R-AZ), Durbin (D-IL), Graham (R-SC), Menendez (D-NJ), Rubio (R-FL), Bennet (D-CO), and Flake (R-AZ) and passed by the Senate 68-32, died when it was not taken up by the House of Representatives.

The bill would have provided a path to citizenship for illegal immigrants already in the United States, contingent on border security and visa tracking improvements. It would also have provided for permanent residence for illegal aliens only after legal aliens receive their permanent residence status, a different citizenship path for agricultural workers, and improved work visa options for low-skilled workers.

In addition, the bill would have expanded and improved the employment verification system for all employers to confirm employee work authorization. Importantly, the bill would have focused on visa backlogs and fast-tracked student visa graduates with advanced STEM degrees (science, technology, engineering, and math).

Would the legislation have cured the situation on our Southern border today? No. It would have made the situation better, though, because of the proposed border security measures in the bill.

It is highly doubtful today's Senate would pass the bill (the House would, I presume), but President Trump would probably not sign it in any case. So what should one do?

Try to resurrect the bill (two of the original senators—McCain and Flake—are no longer in Congress). Implement a "Marshall Plan" for El

Salvador, Guatemala, and Honduras (a major investment of capital in those countries, from which most of the migrants crossing our Southern border come, to shore those countries up, as the United States did in Western Europe following World War II to prevent European countries from falling to communism). Hold asylum hearings at the embassy in the country of origin. And, increase the number of judges who can determine the legitimacy of a person's asylum claim.

As for crossing the border illegally and making the crossing a civil, rather than a criminal, penalty, it is a bad idea. While it is very doubtful the requisite legislation would pass, it is highly likely illegal immigration would increase due to the perceived "open border." As a result, classifying illegal entry into the United States as a civil penalty would be another way Democrats could put Trump back into the White House for a second term.

Finally, abandon the idea of providing illegal immigrants with health insurance. Clearly, we cannot, should not, and will not let a person suffer who illegally crosses the border and becomes sick or injured, but the idea of providing insurance to those who have illegally crossed into the United States makes no sense, morally or politically, when millions of our citizens are either uncovered or covered insufficiently.

As an aside, it is widely—and wrongly—assumed all Latinos will turn out in force to vote Trump out of office. How could any Latino, and any Mexican in particular, vote for Trump after his pejorative comments about them? Easily.

Millions of immigrants from South of the border "stood in line" to gain access to the United States. Why, they may ask, should someone "jump the line" by coming into this country illegally? As a result, despite the hateful rhetoric Trump spews about Latinos, it would not be surprising to see up to 30% of the Latino vote go to Trump.

So, secure the border, end the atrocious policy of separating children from their parents (and putting them in cages), adopt common-sense policies, and implement those policies in a humane way that is in accord with longstanding American values. And, of course, do not take the Latino vote for granted.

REPARATIONS

An issue that has been discussed on various occasions beginning in the 1860s, reparations seems, at best, an unusual item for discussion in a 21st-century presidential campaign. Yes, one can argue all issues warrant an airing. But for an issue, with zero chance of emerging from the legislative process at this time, to receive attention during the Democratic presidential process is troubling, especially since the issue could result in a political backlash.

Let's begin with two obvious statements: African-Americans who came to the United States before emancipation did so in chains; and slavery was an abomination for which there is no justification. None.

Let's add a third, equally obvious, statement, with which no reasonable person should disagree: Native Americans were treated, if anything, even worse than Blacks. After all, the annihilation of people because they were deemed "savages" is an abomination on steroids.

African-Americans were abused horribly. Brought to this country in chains 400 years ago, Blacks have suffered brandings, whippings, rape, and murder.

Other than not being brought to America, though, Native Americans have suffered many of the same abominations. Add to that treatment the fact Indians were slaughtered or given blankets with smallpox. (Even Thomas Jefferson wanted to "extirpate" Indians who provoked attacks on Whites.)

The wrongs done to both African-Americans and Native Americans are beyond dispute. So, if one wrong is to be addressed, what about the other?

Reparations was the concept first discussed by Radical Republicans in 1868. Meant to provide restitution for the indignities suffered by Blacks, it was also believed the funds would give African-Americans a financial base. Less than a decade later, the concept had faded away.

For three decades, Congressman John Conyers championed legislation to form a commission to study the issue of reparations and to develop a formula for providing funds to Black Americans. (The legislation is now being championed by Congresswoman Barbara Lee.)

Reparations are viewed as the way to close the financial gap between Black and White Americans (one estimate has the funding required to eliminate that gap at $17 trillion). Since only about 20% of Whites support the concept, it is hard to see how the issue will gain traction in an election year, regardless of the merits of the concept.

Besides, as noted, as horrific as the treatment of African-Americans has been, it is hard to justify trying to ameliorate their plight while leaving out Native Americans. Moreover, if the argument is financial, the gap between Indians and Whites is equally great.

In financial terms, the family income for Native Americans is roughly 10% higher than for Blacks. On a per capita basis, though, Indians earn less than Blacks and are the poorest ethnic group in the United States.

The financial widening of the gap between Whites and other Americans is both troubling and unsustainable. At the same time, the question is not whether the gap should be discussed in a presidential campaign but whether the specific remedy of reparations should be put forward, since Blacks are certainly not the only group that could make a strong argument for reparations.

GUN CONTROL

Well before El Paso and the planned attack on Mexican-Americans, the United States had been subjected to domestic terrorism. It took, though, the El Paso massacre for the label to be attached to the mass killings of Americans on American soil, since a specific ethnic group was singled out.

Columbine. Aurora. Sandy Hook. Parkland. San Bruno. Nashville. Pittsburgh. Orlando. Las Vegas. El Paso. Dayton. The list goes on and on and on.

One cannot name another country that, faced with the epidemic of mass shootings the United States has endured, has not taken strong action. In fact, other countries have acted after a single incident.

To date, despite our growing list of shootings, we have done nothing in the United States. Well, that is not exactly true: Politicians have always expressed their condolences to and prayers for the victims' families.

Thanks to an outsized impact by the National Rifle Association, and thanks, too, to narrow Supreme Court decisions on just what limitations can be placed on the Second Amendment to the Constitution, the shootings continue. Something must be done. Ninety percent of the US population agrees.

It is hard to believe the ratification of the Second Amendment on December 15, 1791 could lead us to where we as a people now are. Muskets (and rifles, shotguns, and hand guns)? Yes. But assault weapons and unlimited ammunition clips? No.

Mass shootings account for roughly 2% of gun deaths in the United States; the majority of shootings (70%) are suicides. While the answer to death by suicide is a real challenge, dealing with mass shootings is not.

Shouldn't we, as any and every other nation would, address the issue of mass shootings? Shouldn't we seek common-sense approaches to reduce gun violence? The answer seems obvious, although any solution has to take into account the harsh reality that we are a people in love with our guns.

No one is saying guns should be banned. That "solution" is not viable, and it is not necessary. Although gun buyback programs might have some benefit, as a number of cities would argue, guns will not be banned in the United States.

Yet that is precisely the red herring the NRA is waving in front of its members and those whom the NRA supports in Congress. Give an inch, the NRA argues, and we will soon be on a slippery slope that will lead to the banning of all guns in

America. Bull (and most NRA members agree the position is bull)!

Without running into Second Amendment issues, there are reasonable steps that can be taken: red flag laws that identify people who are a danger to others (and themselves); background checks (including closing the loophole for gun show purchases and individual sales, without which red flag laws are meaningless); an assault weapons ban and buyback programs for assault weapons in use; and magazine clip limits.

Of course, with the exception of red flag laws and background checks that can result in the removal of guns from individuals who pose a risk to themselves or others, there will be strong, divergent views. Let's implement these two items, therefore, both of which have overwhelming public support, including from NRA members.

As for other issues that make sense, there are problems. One of those problems is that most assault weapons are nothing more than weapons platforms, on which parts can be easily mixed and matched. So, a non-assault weapon can, fairly simply, be modified with a few tools to become an assault weapon. And, unfortunately, those guns are each year being turned into deadlier and deadlier weapons of death.

Our one attempt at trying to control these weapons of war was the Federal Assault Weapons Ban of 1994. In effect for 10 years, it "sunsetted" in 2004. Importantly, Democrats felt it was the cause of their loss of Congress in 1994. For some presidential candidates, that fear may, unfortunately, still exist.

Gun control opponents argue that guns don't kill, people do. Really?

And what would those gun control opponents have said if the first (official) act of domestic terrorism had come from an Islamic gunman who had targeted Whites, rather than, as in El Paso, a white supremacist who targeted Mexican-Americans? Probably that, if only someone in the crowd had a weapon, the gunman would have been stopped before more carnage occurred.

Well, that argument blew up in El Paso. Texas is a "carry" state, where, undoubtedly, some people in the Walmart store, where the shooting took place, had weapons. Not assault weapons, but guns nevertheless. (And, by the way, there undoubtedly were assault weapons for sale at Walmart, which no one used to stop the gunman, although, to be fair, the rampage was over in seconds.)

Without assault weapons that were designed for the battlefield, people would have a dramatically more difficult time to take the lives of large groups of people. When one lets any and everyone get guns, and when those guns are turned into weapons of war that no civilian has any justified need to use, it is time to act.

Yet taking any guns away from citizens, specifically assault weapons as Beto O'Rourke is proposing, stands no chance of passage. It does, though, stand a great chance of hurting the Democratic presidential nominee in 2020.

Congress and the President need to do something. Ideally, they would pass and sign red flag, expanded background check, assault ban, and ammunition clip legislation. The ideal is not possible, though, not with this President and not with Mitch McConnell running the Senate.

At the very least, red flag and expanded background check legislation should be passed now. Yet even those items will not move forward unless the President signals to McConnell his willingness to sign the legislation—or until we have a new President and a Democratically-controlled Senate.

CLIMATE CHANGE

With 97% of scientists asserting climate change is unequivocal, it is hard to understand how people can deny our climate is changing. Still, despite science's evidence to the contrary, skeptics exist, including, unfortunately, in the Oval Office.

Some of those skeptics seek to point to minor but positive results that could, theoretically, emanate from the looming environmental disaster. Those so-called benefits to our changing climate: agricultural products could be grown where, before, it was too cold (although it takes hundreds of years to create suitable soil for crops, assuming adequate rainfall); fewer people will die in winter because it will not be as cold; and shipping products by sea will be easier with the melting of arctic ice. Really?

Compared to the serious, irreversible effects of climate change, though, these "benefits" seem ridiculous. Among those effects: increased wildfires; less fresh water; increased deaths due to heatwaves; coastal flooding from rising oceans; overflowing rivers from stronger storms; the spread of mosquito-borne diseases; significant loss of animal species (polar bears, for example); the death of healthy trees; the flooding of lowland countries like Bangladesh; military bases that will have to be relocated; and increased conflicts around the world.

Regarding the last point, let's take Africa as an example of how conflicts can occur. With the sands of the Sahara spreading south, there is less ability for nations encroached on by the shifting sands to feed their people. And with less food and water in those countries, the obvious "answer" is to look to neighboring nations for land to appropriate through war.

Aside from this relatively localized situation, there is the effect of climate change on nations and people much further afield. Simply stated, people are being displaced, and climate change has had a role in the displacement.

In the hypothetical African example cited, farmers in sub-Saharan countries who can no longer farm are forced to take their families and move. Alternatively, those farmers may seek a way of existing elsewhere and sending funds to their families back home.

Either way, disruption occurs on both ends. The family disruption is obvious. So, too, is the disruption on the countries to which the refugee farmers migrate, as the millions of refugees entering Europe in the past years demonstrate. While most of the refugees were fleeing conflicts in Iraq, Syria, and Libya, others were simply seeking a better economic life, which, in part, was caused by draught in Africa.

In the United States, which has less than 5% of the world's population but is responsible for roughly 25% of the carbon production that is heating our planet, several Democrats have embraced the Green New Deal. By ending our use of fossil fuels, they believe we can do our part to lessen the effects of climate change; and by developing new industries that use solar and wind energy, they believe we can grow our economy.

It is difficult to see how a Congress, with members representing coal, oil, and gas interests, will want to shutter mining operations throughout the United States. Rather than an all or nothing approach, therefore, an alternative might be to tackle the situation incrementally.

Fewer and fewer countries are interested in using coal because of damage to the environment and the availability of less costly alternatives like natural gas. Yet several states—Kentucky, Ohio, West Virginia, and Wyoming—have significant deposits of and investments in coal and remain "wetted" to coal for the livelihood of their citizens.

What do we do with those states? What do we do with those employed in those fossil-fuel operations? Again, how about an incremental approach that starts with a demonstration project or two?

Take one or two of those states and develop a solar-panel plant at the site of a shuttered coal mine? By retraining coal miners, who otherwise would be out of work if the coal mine were shuttered, those miners could be gainfully employed in the community in which they now live. Both the local economy and the environment would benefit.

Rather than seeking a way to address climate change, the Arsonist-in-Chief's approach to the environment in general and climate change in particular has been four-fold: Deny climate change exists; withdraw from the Paris Climate Agreement (adopted by consensus by 196 countries); gut the Environmental Protection Agency by putting a petroleum industry lobbyist in charge of the agency; and weaken the protection of the Endangered Species Act to allow for more drilling and mining.

Fortunately, the rest of the world is moving in a different direction. Renewable energy has become the cheapest form of power in two-thirds of the world. By 2050, forecasts show that renewable energy and natural gas will have forced coal to all but disappear.

Historically, from Theodore Roosevelt to Richard Nixon, Republicans have been good stewards of the environment. But that was a long time ago. Trump is unconcerned about that history, the state of the environment, or the reality of what is happening across the globe, since he is only interested in "winning" now—even if it means losing later.

TAXES

No one likes to pay taxes. They are, however, the way this country's government and its programs are financed.

Until 1862, there was no federal income tax in the United States. Instead, the government funded its limited expenses through excise taxes (taxes on products like alcohol, fuel, and tobacco), custom duties, public land sales, and tariffs.

To finance the Civil War, a federal tax was instituted. A decade later, the tax was allowed to lapse. Then, in 1913, the 16th Amendment was passed, which again created a federal income tax.

The federal income tax was meant to be a progressive tax. As incomes rose, so did the top marginal rate at which individuals would be taxed.

At its height, in the 1950s and 1960s, the top marginal tax rate exceeded 90%. In the 1980s, Ronald Reagan slashed taxes; today, the top marginal rate is 37%.

Yet, perhaps surprising to some, the 1950s and 1960s were great decades for the United States economy. Despite extremely high marginal tax rates, the American economy boomed and the middle class was born.

As a result of lower tax rates during the Reagan Administration, there was less revenue for the federal government. Two things (at least) happened: the government went further into debt (the debt now exceeds $22 trillion), and it had less revenue to tackle important projects, like infrastructure.

Under Trump, taxes were reduced further—to no one's benefit other than the rich. His claim was the sweeping tax legislation was "a tax bill for the middle class. It's a tax bill for jobs. It's going to bring a lot of companies in. It's a tax bill for business, which is going to create jobs." Only it wasn't, and it hasn't.

The consensus is that 83% of the benefits went to the top 1% of taxpayers in this country. Although there were, in fact, minor benefits to the other 99% of taxpayers, the benefits of Trump's tax bill clearly were not equally distributed.

Particularly pernicious, but politically shrewd, was the formula architects of the legislation put in place. Keeping (very) questionable practices like carried interest in place for the rich, it capped the deduction for state and local taxes at $10,000, thereby putting a financial hit on states (almost all of which voted Democratic in 2016) that had high taxes.

Ironically, high-tax states are net exporters of tax revenue to those states that have low state and local taxes. And which are those states? "Red" states that voted for Trump. So, in effect, Red states are financially supported by Blue states, and the taxpayers in Blue states pay even more under the Trump tax bill by being able to deduct less on their federal tax returns.

Fair tax legislation is meant to be just that—fair. Since the implementation of the federal income tax in 1916, fairness was the lynchpin of the tax system. Yet, the Trump tax legislation is anything but fair.

At some point, there will be a backlash, perhaps a pitchfork rebellion, because the gap between rich and poor continues to widen. Already several Democratic presidential candidates are calling for higher taxes.

Which brings us back to the days of Presidents Eisenhower and John Kennedy. During their administrations, when taxes were more than double today's top marginal rate, the government had the revenue to accomplish big things. Infrastructure. Putting a man on the moon. And, yes, fighting the Cold War.

Unfortunately, we now live in an age of instant gratification. Sacrificing for tomorrow, which means for our children's and grandchildren's future, seems no longer to be part of the national vision. Instead, by increasing debt, we are mortgaging that future.

As a result, we are doing less because we have less—less revenue with which to tackle big projects and big ideas. In fact, other than entitlement programs and the military, we are doing very little.

No president or presidential candidate will want to tackle the issue of higher taxes, but not for the reason one might expect. By calling for higher income taxes and by talking of increasing the capital gains tax, it will not just be the rich who will be impacted. The middle class, the shrinking middle class, will also bear a burden, and that message is not one politicians, if they even understand the issue, will want to carry.

INFRASTRUCTURE

For anyone who has been lucky enough to have traveled to other countries, one thing is readily apparent: Our infrastructure is closer to a developing than a developed country. To address the issue, the United States would need to invest roughly $2 trillion beyond the projected investment we are planning to make over the next 10 years.

Given the expenditures we have incurred in Afghanistan and Iraq, the reduced revenue from the 2017 tax bill, and the magnitude of the cost of some of the Democratic candidates' proposals, the additional $2 trillion is an unrealistic investment. Something has to give if we are to upgrade, modernize, and replace our existing airports, bridges, roads, and water systems.

Alternatively, additional revenue has to be raised. The most logical approach would be to increase taxes, which is not a particularly good posture to take in an election year.

But other suggestions have been proposed to address the serious problems we face. With local and state authorities also stretched thin, new thinking is required to deal with serious issues like the water crisis in Flint, Michigan, where nearly three years after lead was found in the local water system, people are still drinking bottled water. (And now the lead-in-water problem has "migrated" to Newark, New Jersey.)

Among the ideas that have been suggested are infrastructure bonds, faster permitting of projects to cut down on cost, developing an accurate list of deferred maintenance projects, and public-private partnerships to spread the risk and tackle needed projects more quickly.

Ironically, none of these ideas is being discussed seriously by presidential candidates. They need to be.

How many bridges have to collapse, how many children need to suffer from lead poisoning, how many accidents have to occur before we move forward on these pressing issues? What are we presently doing that we would be willing to give up to insure infrastructure progress? And what are we willing to do to revise the tax code to make sure we do not become a third-world country infrastructure-wise?

Doing everything we now do and adding much-needed initiatives with the revenue the government is now taking in is impossible. We need either to raise additional revenue or reduce what we are presently doing, or we have to become used to being, so far as our infrastructure is concerned, a country more often seen on the African or South American continents.

NATIONAL DEBT

Few people seem to understand the difference between federal deficits and the national debt. The former refers to the annual budget; the latter to the accumulation of federal deficits over the years.

Most people's eyes glaze over when the subject of the national debt arises. They should not, since the size of our national debt has an important impact on our economy.

As the national debt increases, the government has to increase interest rates to pay those willing to purchase our debt. As those interest payments go up, there is less money available for activities—infrastructure, for example—that have a positive effect on the nation's economy.

In addition, the government's creditworthiness comes into play. With an increase in the national debt, the question of the ability of the government to repay that debt comes into play.

Of course, there are good reasons for the national debt to rise. The largest increase in the country's debt occurred during Franklin Delano Roosevelt's presidency. However, the Great Depression and World War II were the reasons for the national debt's growth, as World War I was for the growth of the debt under Woodrow Wilson.

No one can argue with the necessity of spending beyond America's income levels in times of crisis. Providing for wars fits that description; so, too, do depressions and other economic stress periods like the financial crisis of 2007-2008.

One can take issue, though, with the rise in public debt in the 1980s, when Ronald Reagan cut tax rates and increased military spending and when the national debt more than tripled. And one certainly can, and should, take issue with the Trump tax cuts that, in addition to disproportionately benefitting the wealthiest Americans, slashed corporate tax rates and dropped tax revenue from corporations by more than 30%.

Another way of looking at the national debt is to measure the debt burden as a percentage of the gross domestic product (GDP), the total value of goods produced and services provided in the country in one year. The measurement is not pretty, with debt held by the public growing from roughly 35% of GDP in 2000 to 96% of GDP today.

The national debt can grow, and the percentage of debt to GDP can fall, if the economy grows. Conversely, the national debt can decline but the percentage of GDP can grow if the economy stalls.

By increasing the national debt, the United States is placing limits on its future, since continued growth in the national debt is not sustainable. Again, we should not be mortgaging the future of our children and grandchildren by ducking difficult decisions today. And yet, that is precisely what we are doing.

TARIFFS

Tariffs have always been with us. From our very early days as a republic, tariffs were employed to protect our infant industries.

George Washington, Thomas Jefferson, Abraham Lincoln, and Theodore Roosevelt, among other presidents, were all strong proponents of tariffs. In the words of Roosevelt: "Great prosperity in this country has always come under a protective tariff."

With our history in support of tariffs, why is anyone questioning what Trump is doing today? There are (at least) two answers: First, for Republicans, the policy of tariffs reverses a decades-long tradition in favor of free trade; and second, the cost to consumers and taxpayers of imported goods is great.

In announcing his Executive Order to place tariffs on aluminum and steel from Canada, China, the European Union, and Mexico, Trump went to (economic) war with the world. (In fact, only two steel-producing countries were exempt.)

So far as Chinese goods are concerned, the self-described "tariff man" claimed billions of dollars would flow to the Treasury Department. Trump is right, but at a high cost to all Americans.

Although some of the tariff's cost will come from the Chinese government, most will not. That is not how tariffs work.

When goods are imported into the United States, it is the importers who pay the tariff, which they have to do within a specified period of time (usually within 10 days of the goods clearing customs). A portion of that cost is borne by the suppliers.

Perhaps the suppliers may decide to offer importers a discount that, indirectly, offsets the cost of the tariff. Or perhaps suppliers may conclude it is better to run the risk of a tariff-free source of the manufactured goods being developed from another country.

Unless suppliers provide importers with a discount, though, it is the consumer who will bear the burden of the tariff's higher prices. Even if the importer accepts lower profit margins for a while or cuts costs (by lowering wages or laying workers off), consumers will, ultimately, bear the cost. Already, the price of certain products manufactured in China (washing machines, for example) have gone up double-digits. Even Trump acknowledged the cost to consumers, when he delayed the implementation of his newest round of tariffs on Chinese products until December, 2019, so those tariffs would not have a negative impact on consumers at Christmastime.

Then there is the prospect of a lost market. While the "tariff man" has committed to provide American soybean farmers a dollar for each dollar in tariffs placed by China in retaliation on the importation of US soybeans, China is now looking elsewhere.

Brazil, a major grower of soybeans, is stepping into the gap produced by the tariffs on soybeans. Will the American soybean grower lose its Chinese market forever?

In our founding days, and at times thereafter, tariffs were justified. Despite China's massive trade surplus with the United States, which is in large part a result of consumer demand, it is hard to see how the "tariff man's" approach will cause American consumers, manufacturers, and producers anything but heartache in the long run.

STUDENT DEBT

We have a student-debt crisis. With student debt now exceeding $1.5 trillion, how could one call it anything but a crisis?

Interest accrues on student debt when a loan is taken out. Moreover, unlike debt in general, student debt cannot be eradicated by a student or graduate declaring bankruptcy.

The growth in student debt is directly tied to two factors—escalating college costs and stagnant wages. While several dozen colleges and universities have sufficient capital (endowment) to provide the requisite funds for students to attend their institution and graduate without any debt (or, at least, any significant debt), 99% of institutions cannot do so.

So what is the solution? Some Democrats want to provide free tuition to all students attending state colleges and universities. Others want to cancel all outstanding student debt. Neither is a good idea.

Why? Because nothing is free. Someone always has to pay. The question is who? In the case of "free" tuition, it is the public, through increased taxes, that pays.

College tuition is "free" in a number of European countries, but a significantly lower percentage of students go to college in those nations, and the tax rates in Europe are 20% to 60% higher than in the United States. Importantly, those countries have few, if any, private colleges and universities.

Aside from the fact free-tuition proponents make no distinction between wealthy students and those requiring assistance to attend college (which seems foolish), there is the law of unintended consequences. Were this program to be in place, it would put tremendous pressure on private colleges (many of which are barely financially viable), with students who might otherwise attend those colleges seeking admission to "free" state institutions.

If that pressure results in colleges closing (which it undoubtedly would), their students would be forced to go elsewhere. As a result, state institutions would have to add buildings and staff to accommodate the increase in the student body size. In other words, the cost to taxpayers would go up.

Despite cost escalation during the past decades, demand has also gone up. From a financial point of view, high school graduates want a college degree because, over their working lifetime, they will earn nearly twice as much as a high school graduate, thereby justifying the daunting cost of attending college.

With their debt burdens attached to their diploma, though, college graduates are sometimes forced to make career choices for financial, not personally fulfilling, reasons. In addition, with less disposable income, college graduates' life choices are negatively impacted, with, for instance, the possibility of home ownership and resources for starting a business or another venture significantly lessened.

In the past, the government has provided incentives, in the form of cancelable loans, for those entering certain professions or working in specified geographical areas. So have some colleges by providing loans that would be canceled for those entering broadly-defined public service.

Encouraging graduates into certain fields where shortages exist makes sense. So, too, does providing incentives for work in rural or inner city areas that need people in certain professions.

For those with student debt, one option to reduce a loan recipient's cost would be to have interest on that debt assumed by the government, since an educated populace is in its best interest. Alternatively, since employers also benefit from that educated workforce, adding to the corporate tax rate to cover the cost of that interest would also seem reasonable.

But there is another approach that would benefit this nation—tying together student debt and national service. The idea is hardly novel, since states today offer free tuition for veterans. As noted, we have in the past provided "free" education to doctors or teachers who went into certain fields of study or agreed to work in specific geographical areas (and, of course, we had, from 1944 to 1956, the Servicemen's Readjustment Act of 1944 or "G.I." Bill, and we have today the Post-9/11 G.I. Bill).

We can (and should) go further, though. By providing "cancelable" loans for those engaged in the military or public service broadly defined, we would both help heal divisions by having people of all backgrounds and ethnicities work together, provide for the cost of a person's education, and make our communities and nation stronger.

The same approach could be tied to debt that has been accumulated by older graduates. No, those students (long graduated) need not switch careers. But they could be part of an imaginative program that would allow them to cancel their debt over a period of time through volunteer work. It would be a lengthy process, but such an approach could work. Besides, what is the harm in trying a new approach to solve a very serious problem?

Let's not look for quick fixes that are problematic, though. And let's not abrogate personal responsibility when tackling this difficult issue.

Nothing is truly free, and nothing should be made free after the fact. If someone has incurred an obligation, that obligation should be met (although one might rightly ask how many corporations were able to walk away from their obligations during the 2007-8 financial crisis).

With every so-called "free" program, there are costs. While free tuition sounds great, it isn't. (Well, perhaps for the recipient, but not for taxpayers and not for society.)

Clearly, though, $1.5 trillion in student debt (which is growing annually) is an unsustainable situation. We need to do something, but "free" education and the cancellation of existing debt is not that something.

FOREIGN POLICY

Ever since the end of World War II, the United States has played "the" leadership role in the world. By bringing together allies, the United States has, for nearly 75 years, fostered territorial integrity, the peaceful resolution of disputes, and a respect for international law and norms.

That role, which most observers would agree has been in the national interest of the United States, is now being undermined. From his questioning of the North Atlantic Treaty Organization to his attacks on our longstanding allies around the world, Trump has upended a decades-old policy that has served the United States and the world well.

Yes, there have clearly been problems and serious "mistakes"—Vietnam and Iraq come quickly to mind. But, although the role the United States has played served its own national interest, America has defended democracy, freedom, and human rights worldwide to the benefit of millions of people across the globe.

The question: Should the role the United States played for more than seven decades be its role going forward? Or, stated differently, should America, at the expense of universal values (democracy, freedom, and human rights), pursue solely its own interests?

During the past three years, traditional allies have been forced to rethink their reliance on the United States. How could they not do so?

With Trump trumpeting America First and questioning the value of historic relationships (his insistence that NATO members fulfill their financial obligations is right, though), multilateral and regional trade agreements (withdrawing from the Trans-Pacific Partnership and the Iran nuclear agreement and, instead, wanting to negotiate new agreements with trading partners), and efforts to defend freedom abroad, it would be diplomatic malpractice for them to do otherwise. America First might, ultimately, lead to America alone.

Of course, there are instances where Trump has sought to work with other nations. Those efforts, from asking the Australian Prime Minister to look into the Mueller inquiry's origins to the pressuring of Ukraine's President to gather dirt on the Biden family in exchange for military aid, may very well result in Trump's impeachment (it should).

In the aftermath of the drone attack on Saudi Arabia's oil fields, the United States has also sought support from our allies in challenging Iran.

In the past, those allies would quickly have lined up with America.

After the United States' exit from the Iranian nuclear agreement, though (which our allies continue to support), will they join with America in a showdown with Iran? And with the barrage of lies emanating from the White House, will our allies believe what Trump tells them about Iran's involvement in the Saudi attack?

Then there is China. Given its population, military, and growing economy (which will soon be the largest in the world), and given the investments it is making around the globe, China will present increasing challenges to the United States. And to meet those challenges, America will need to work closely with its Asian and European allies, since the United States cannot meet those challenges by itself.

Next there is Russia. Operating almost as a "Siberian" president, Trump has never uttered a negative word regarding Vladimir Putin or Russia. As a result, it is hard to conclude anything other than that Putin has dirt on Trump, Trump prefers dictators to democrats, Trump continues to want to build a Moscow tower, or Trump knows Putin, through the use of various platforms, helped engineer his election victory.

Finally, so far as the Saudi killing of journalist Jamal Khashoggi is concerned, the current resident of 1600 Pennsylvania Avenue said nothing. Since Trump is generally incapable of remaining silent, his reaction was particularly surprising. Perhaps it should not have been.

Given the Trump affinity for authoritarian rulers, Trump's silence could have been nothing more than his siding with yet another dictator. Alternatively, the silence might have been motivated by greed, since the Saudis have long invested heavily in Trump properties. Whatever the reason, Trump's silence on the Khashoggi murder contrasts sharply (and negatively) with the moral stance past American presidents have taken.

A legitimate and thoughtful debate over the future role of American power is appropriate. Unfortunately, rather than have a real debate, though, we—and the rest of the world—are forced to react to a daily barrage of unpresidential tweets masquerading as foreign policy.

MILITARY

Since the end of World War II, the United States has served as the policeman of the world. It is a role that, increasingly, has come to be questioned.

Following the collapse of the Soviet Union and the end of the Cold War, the United States found itself the world's sole "super power." Suddenly, the security needs of the country were dramatically changed. With that change, America's military requirements needed to be reassessed.

While the primary focus of the military is to defend the United States from attack, it also has the obligation to protect Americans abroad, our allies, and our ability to use, without impediments, international air, sea, and space corridors. Inherent in those objectives is the ability to defend the United States and our varied interests and to deter those who seek to challenge those interests.

For years, the focus was on being able to fight successfully wars on two fronts. Today, there are questions as to our ability to do so.

There are also questions as to what we need to do to win in combat. Instead of focusing on numbers—of planes, ships, ground forces, missiles, and nuclear weapons—the military today is relying less on those numbers than in developing the requisite strategy to win a combat engagement.

From a budgetary standpoint, the pressures on the military (and all parties that have a stake in the budget) are great. The military believes it needs continued growth in the base budget of at least 3% above the rate of inflation to preserve the advantages we presently enjoy.

Republicans have long championed expenditures on the military, rather than on social programs. Today is no different.

Of course, we need a strong military. But military expenditures need to be closely monitored. Unless the United States is engaged in an ongoing war, there needs to be a balancing of domestic and international (military) interests. And there needs to be, too, a recognition the House of Representatives has the "power of the purse."

Incredibly, the power of the purse, too, is now a casualty of the Trump presidency. Even more incredible, the Supreme Court has sanctioned Trump's siphoning of funds for his "big, beautiful" wall.
Seeking to build his wall to fulfill his campaign pledge, Trump is moving funds from Congressionally-approved military expenditures to the building of sections of the wall. Either those

approved expenditures were unnecessary in the first place, which is another issue, or important military objectives were weakened by the action. (Besides, whatever happened to getting Mexico to pay for the wall?)

We should not engage—we never should have engaged—in frivolous military actions or in wars of regime change. As is painfully apparent with the conflict in Iraq, those wars never end well. So, Congress needs to monitor every situation involving the use of force.

Afghanistan presents a very different problem. Since it was the staging ground for the attack on 9/11, our action there was certainly justified.

Whether an 18-year (and counting) war effort in Afghanistan is justified, though, is another question. For those who gave life or limb during the conflict, simply pulling out is not the answer. Neither is staying in Afghanistan forever. To date, no one has come up with a solution that addresses both of these points.

So far as the military budget is concerned, one recent suggestion is to have it indexed to a percent of the gross domestic product. But the percent of the budget tied to the military does not make America more secure. And making the military budget larger does not necessarily ensure a safer United States, either.

Bigger investments in the military are not necessarily the answer. Instead, those investments should be smarter and reflect the reality that the wars of the past will not be the wars of the future.

As for whether the United States should continue to be the policeman of the world, a qualified "yes" would seem appropriate. With proper Congressional involvement in any decision before American forces are committed to a war in a far-off part of the world, and with adherence to our constitutional prescriptions, the answer is "yes," if we want to remain true to the principles on which this nation was founded.

Yet, there is another issue regarding the military that must be addressed—the disgraceful way in which former members of the military are "reintegrated" into society. When the one-half of one percent of America's population that serves in the military returns home, the 99% that have been protected by them have a moral obligation to help veterans readjust.

From health care issues (delays in treatment, post-traumatic stress disorder, and suicide) to homelessness to unemployment, we need to fulfill our obligation of helping veterans who have fought

to protect us. To date, we have failed that
obligation, and we have failed it miserably.

THE JUDICIAL SYSTEM

Elections have consequences. Those consequences are huge.

We do not have to look far for proof of the validity of this obvious statement. The 2016 election provides that proof.

The roughly 77,000 people who, together apparently with assistance from the Russians, made Trump our 45th president, were vastly outnumbered by those who chose to stay home. And by staying home, whether because of disgust with the Democratic National Committee's gamesmanship in the 2016 Clinton-Sanders primary or of being misled by Russian messaging during the general election, the non-voters handed the Republicans (and the Russians) and the American electorate a fake president.

Almost immediately, the Antonin Scalia/Merrick Garland seat on the Supreme Court was filled by Neil Gorsuch; then Brett Kavanaugh was elevated to the Supreme Court. Both appointments came via recommendations from the Federalist Society and both would have been nominated regardless of which Republican president was in office (although, as president, Trump got credit from conservatives for these appointments).

Of course, it is not only the Supreme Court that has been changed. So, too, have all of the lower federal courts.

With more than 150 appointments (and counting) to the district courts and courts of appeals, federal courts have been changed for a generation—at least. Elections do have consequences, and, for those with a different legal perspective than the hardline conservatives appointed, the 2016 election had negative consequences.

Critical rights have come under attack by those appointed to the courts during the first years of Trump's term in office. So, too, has the rule of law itself.

From his earliest days in office, Trump has shown nothing but contempt for the rule of law. By attacking judges who disagree with him, demanding loyalty from those in the law enforcement community, threatening investigations into members of the press and those opposed to his policies, and undermining independent investigations (as the Mueller Report makes patently clear), this Siberian president has done more to undermine the legal norms on which our system is based than Vladimir Putin could have ever accomplished through his operatives. (Then again, one could almost make the case that Trump is a Putin operative.). Credit should always be given when and where it is deserved. And the "credit" for allowing Trump to make the judicial appointments he has made goes to Mitch McConnell.

During the Obama presidency, McConnell employed the filibuster to prevent the confirmation of a number of judicial appointments made by Obama. The result: Trump had twice as many openings on the federal bench as Obama had when he entered office, and McConnell filled those positions with names supplied by the Federalist Society.

One often hears or reads about judicial end-runs. Here one saw it clearly.

As a case in point, the Affordable Care Act, as already noted, is, yet again, facing a legal challenge. Although Republicans were unable to kill it in Congress, they may be able to do so through the legal process with the recent appointments that have been made, especially, but not exclusively, to the Supreme Court.

The ongoing legal attack on the Affordable Care Act (Obamacare) is of import to millions of Americans. But so, too, is the question of a woman's right to choose, which, on almost a monthly basis, is undergoing legal challenges that will also make it to the Supreme Court.

One idea floated by some Democrats is to "pack" the court. In other words, the idea is to increase the size of the Supreme Court (last changed in 1869) to circumvent the fact that conservatives now control the court. Last tried by Franklin Delano Roosevelt, packing the court—which FDR quickly gave up—is a bad idea, since the door would then be opened for Republicans to follow suit in the future.

A better idea—win elections. Elections do have consequences, Democrats—for all Americans!

CRIMINAL JUSTICE REFORM

In the United States, 2.1 million people are incarcerated. With that number, the United States has the distinction of having 35% more people in prison than the 1.5 million incarcerated in China's prisons—and China, the country second to the United States in the number of people incarcerated, has a population five times greater than the United States.

Aside from the number of people in prison, the United States has the dubious distinction of housing more prisoners as a percentage of population than any other country in the world. Americans have a prison rate population 20% higher than Russia, which sits in second place worldwide.

With the passage of the First Step Act, bipartisan legislation signed into law by the Trump, the United States prison population will be reduced by roughly 10%. The legislation eases punitive federal measures and allows thousands of people to earn earlier release from prison.

By reducing the disparity between crack and powdered cocaine, avoiding mandatory minimum sentences, allowing judges to impose a 25-year sentence rather than life imprisonment under the "three-strikes" rule, and allowing prisoners to earn good-time credits, the First Step Act makes early release from prison possible.

The basis for the legislation is premised on research that shows longer prison sentences do not combat crime. In fact, longer prison sentences may increase crime, since prisons serve as laboratories for crime.

With 87% of prisoners held in state prison, though, the impact of the legislation will be small. With more and more states legalizing the use of marijuana, however, it is easy to see how state incarceration should also decline.

In any case, though, a first step is better than no step. After all, despite some senators claiming we are "under-incarcerated," we should not be very happy leading the world in the number and percentage of people held in prison.

A WOMAN'S RIGHT TO CHOOSE

The 1973 ruling in <u>Roe v. Wade</u> seemed to end, once and for all, the question of whether and when a woman had the right to terminate her pregnancy. But 2019 is not 1973, and the Supreme Court today is not the court that gave us that landmark decision.

In 2019, a number of states passed fetal heartbeat bills. Undoubtedly, as those bills are challenged in court, the Supreme Court will become the final arbiter once again—and, perhaps, again and again, since states are continuously seeking a way to limit, and ultimately reverse, <u>Roe v. Wade</u>.

While <u>Roe</u> is ostensibly settled law, it is unsettling to read, almost on a weekly basis, of restrictive laws being passed by legislatures in the Midwest and South. The laws run the gamut from requiring waiting periods for those wanting an abortion, to banning surgical procedures, to preventing state funds from being used to conduct abortions, to nearly total bans on abortions.

In "normal" times, citing <u>Roe,</u> the Supreme Court would strict down all of these attempts to limit a woman's constitutional right to an abortion. But these are not normal times, and the court system is becoming increasingly "conservative."

Based on the 14th Amendment's right to privacy, a woman's right to choose is now under assault in a way it has not been since the landmark 1973 decision. Every one of the new attempts to limit abortions is a clear violation of the main tenet of Roe: Abortion cannot be restricted before the fetus is viable, since an unborn child is not a person.

Therein, of course, lies the argument on which those opposed to abortion are pinning their hopes. If the fetus' viability is the litmus test for Roe, does the technology that has been developed since 1973 change the definition of when life begins?

Although the majority (roughly 60%) of Americans believe abortion should be legal during the first trimester, the percentage drops off significantly after the first three months. And less than 15% of those surveyed believe it should be permitted in the final trimester.

The issue of abortion involves morality, as well as legality. Because of the religious and deeply personal questions involved, the Roe opinion was based on the Supreme Court's citing of the 14th Amendment's right of privacy.

What the Supreme Court will ultimately do is open to debate. It is hard to see, despite its obviously more conservative nature today than in 1973, how the court will totally reverse its thinking from nearly 50 years ago. Then again, one could have said the same thing about <u>Plessy v. Ferguson,</u> an 1896 decision supporting the concept of "separate but equal" that was overturned 58 years later by <u>Brown v. Board of Education of Topeka</u>.

Importantly, for Democrats who want to see a new occupant at 1600 Pennsylvania Avenue in 2021, there needs to be respect both for those who believe life begins at conception and those who think a woman should always have the right to choose what to do with her body. Of all the issues facing Democrats today, keeping both of these parties in the same tent may be the most challenging of all.

VOTING RIGHTS

One issue that should have long passed from the legal and political scene is voter suppression. It hasn't.

In 1965, Congress passed the Voting Rights Act. Its purpose: to insure state and local governments do not pass laws or policies whose sole purpose is to deny Americans the right to vote based on race.

For 48 years, the legislation remained in place. However, in Shelby County (Alabama) v. Holder, the Supreme Court scrapped a section of the Voting Rights Act, which required states with a history of racial discrimination to get federal approval from either the Justice Department or the federal courts for any changes to their voting laws.

In a 5-4 decision, the court in Shelby decided the formula to ascertain which states needed preclearance to be too broad. Importantly, it did not say preclearance, in and of itself, was unconstitutional.

No sooner had the Supreme Court issued its decision in Shelby than other states immediately passed restrictive voting legislation. From Alabama to Georgia to Mississippi, from North Carolina to Texas, from Indiana to Kansas, from Tennessee to Virginia to Wisconsin, legislatures put in place strict photo ID laws, restrictions on early registration, early voting cutbacks, and laws making it harder to register (and to stay registered). In the past, most of those states would have needed federal approval for these restrictive laws.

The sacredness of the ballot should be sacrosanct. Unfortunately, it is not.

Blatant attempts to silence the voices of Americans by preventing them from voting is, at best, unpatriotic. With American troops having lost their lives around the globe to give people the right to vote, it is amazing there are those who seek to prevent fellow Americans from exercising their rights in this country. Yet, through the purging of voter names from voter registration rolls, polling station closures, and strict photo ID laws, that is precisely what they are doing for purely political purposes.

As for whom these "laws" affect, the answer is clear: those without permanent addresses or a need for photo IDs. And who are those individuals— Native Americans who live on reservations without street addresses and African-Americans.

Amazing, too, is the fact so few Americans choose to vote. In 2016, roughly 56% of eligible voters bothered to cast their ballots. Twenty-five other developed countries had a higher percentage of eligible voters cast a ballot.

Voter suppression and voter lethargy are both stunning and depressing: stunning that Americans would seek to prevent fellow Americans from voting so they could advance a particular agenda; and depressing that so many Americans willingly forego a right that others have sacrificed life and limb to give people around the world.

A final comment regards voter fraud, a theme the present occupant of 1600 Pennsylvania Avenue continuously repeats. Yes, voter fraud exists—in an infinitesimally tiny way.

According to a Washington Post study, during the period of 2000-2014, there were 31 fraudulent ballots cast—out of a total of roughly one billion ballots. It is time to jettison partisan rhetoric. Rather than following Trump's fraudulent cry of voter fraud, let's address the real problem in America today—too few people voting and too much voter suppression.

CAMPAIGN FINANCING

Since the mid-nineteenth century, there have been attempts to regulate campaign financing. Those attempts have had, over the years, no real success.

The Federal Election Campaign Act of 1971 required candidates to disclose the sources of campaign contributions, together with how those funds were expended. Amended three years later, the revised legislation placed statutory limits on individual campaign contributions and established the Federal Election Commission to oversee the implantation of the act.

The 1974 Amendments sought to limit individual contributions to $1000 and political action committee contributions to $5000. Two years later, the contribution limits were struck down by the Supreme Court.

It took another 15 years for action to be taken to try to remedy the situation. In 2002, a bipartisan effort, led by Senators McCain and Feingold (D-WI), resulted in the Bipartisan Campaign Reform Act of 2002.

The Bipartisan Campaign Reform Act attempted to limit unregulated contributions ("soft money") to national political parties. In addition, it limited corporate and union contributions to fund ads within 60 days of an election or 30 days of a primary.

First narrowed in <u>Federal Election Commission v. Wisconsin Right to Life (2007)</u>, the corporate and union spending limitations were struck down in 2010 in the bizarre case of <u>Citizens United v. Federal Election Commission</u>. As a result of <u>Citizens United,</u> the attempt to stem the role of money in elections suffered a major setback.

In <u>Citizens United</u>, another 5-4 decision, the Supreme Court concluded that corporations and unions were to be treated as individuals and permitted, under the First Amendment, to free speech protections. In the court's view, the government could not restrict independent expenditures for political communications by them.

Speaking for the minority, the recently deceased John Paul Stevens argued the Court's ruling represented "a rejection of the common sense of the American people, who have recognized a need to prevent corporations from undermining self-government."
Corporations and unions—and their lobbyists—won. Unlimited election spending by them, and by the super political action committees the decision spawned, gave special interests even more power.

Yes, elections do have consequences. As the 2020 elections loom, we should all be painfully aware of that fact.

THE ECONOMY

In a presidential election year, the economy has long been thought to be controlling. If there is full employment, rising wages, low inflation, a rising stock market, and economic growth, a president seeking reelection is in good political shape. In other words, if individuals can say they are better off than they were four years earlier, a president running for reelection is in a strong position.

Trump supposedly has those factors going for him. If so, why is the 2020 election in doubt?

And why is the present occupant of 1600 Pennsylvania Avenue constantly attacking his appointment to head the Federal Reserve, Jerome Powell, and pushing him to lower interest rates? Perhaps because he knows the economy is not what he claims it to be.

Let's be clear: The United States economy has grown every month following the Great Recession of 2008. As a result, we are in the longest economic expansion in American history. Importantly, though, as a result of the aftermath of the 2008 housing crisis, the expansion has been weaker than past expansions, with the cumulative gross domestic product growth aggregating 25 percent during that period.

During that same period, the unemployment rate has dropped continuously and significantly. From a high of 10% in 2009, the rate, as Trump likes to claim, has dropped to 3.6%, which is the lowest rate in 50 years. Yet, despite impressive job growth, the job growth rate is less than in previous recoveries.

The expansion keeps moving along, though. In part, it has been aided by the 2017 tax cuts and, of course, deregulation.

A lowering of interest rates, as Trump keeps pushing the Federal Reserve to do, would, therefore, hardly seem necessary or appropriate. With mountains of cash, corporations do not need lower interest rates to get them to invest.

Besides, isn't the United States economy great? At least that is what Trump repeatedly tells us.

Upon passage of the 2017 tax legislation, Trump crowed:
"It'll be fantastic for the middle-income people and for jobs, most of all ... I think we could go to 4%, 5% or even 6% [GDP growth], ultimately. We are back. We are really going to start to rock."

During the first quarter of 2019, growth was just over 3%; the second quarter was 2.1%. Wage growth, which has been stagnant for far too long (and whose lack of growth helped Trump "win" the presidency in 2016), has only moved marginally, despite the 2017 tax cuts.

As noted by famed economists like Joseph Stieglitz, the United States should be firing on all economic fronts as a result of the stimulus of the $1.5-2 trillion Trump tax cuts, the $300 billion expenditures to avert a 2018 government shutdown, and the $320 billion in expenditures to avoid another government shutdown. It isn't.

We have, though, increased our debt obligations 20% during the Trump presidency, despite the fact Trump claimed he was going to wipe out our national debt. And with the rise in our debt level during good times, what will he—and the Federal Reserve—do when the inevitable economic downturn occurs?

The economy is certainly working well for wealthy Americans. Not so for the rest of America. Again, as Stieglitz has noted, incomes have been stagnating, infrastructure has been decaying, middle-income Americans have been paying more in taxes, and the economy has weakened as income is redistributed to the top, thereby leaving those below with less money to spend.

One other note: Trump keeps equating the economy and the stock market, two very different animals. To the extent Trump wants to hang his hat on stock market gains, though, he needs to understand, as presumably he does not, the run-up under Barack Obama was twice what it was under him.

According to Fortune Magazine, the Dow grew by 50.6% under Obama during his first two years, and 25.2% under Trump during a two-year period. Since a majority of Americans (54%) are invested in the stock market (largely through their retirement funds), a downturn of the market in an election year would presumably have an impact on the 2020 election.

Moreover, for Republicans who think the stock market does better under Republicans than Democrats, they are wrong. According to a recent Forbes analysis, since 1929 the market has grown, on average (during a four-year presidential term), 16.61% under Republicans and 57.44% under Democrats. Although a variety of factors are responsible for those numbers, the market has performed demonstrably better when Democratic presidents were in office.

ENERGY

Coal, gas, and oil have long been an important part of the American economic landscape. Our energy future, though, lies not in these areas, at least not in coal and oil. Yet, rather than look to the renewable energy of the 21st century, Trump has sought to turn the clock back to the early 20th century.

Smart politics? Perhaps. Dumb policy? Undoubtedly. Then again, when one's focus is transactional, one only looks to today, not tomorrow—and the present occupant of 1600 Pennsylvania Avenue is as transactional a person as there is.

Trump campaigned against the scientific community and promised to repeal any regulation that impeded the exploration and mining of energy, that is of coal, gas, and oil. He has, foolishly, kept that promise.

Ten years ago, coal industry officials were predicting that global demand for coal would grow faster than oil, natural gas, nuclear, and renewable energy combined. Yet today, renewable energy supplies more power to America's grid than coal, and it is doing so because renewable energy has become the most profitable part of the power business.

Unfortunately, facts—real facts—do not matter to the Arsonist-in-Chief. He has rescinded the Environmental Protection Agency's Clean Power Plan and the Interior Department's moratorium on new coal mining on public land; he has withdrawn from the 196 country-approved Paris agreement; he has revived the Keystone XL pipeline; he has increased the leasing of public land by oil and gas companies, including opening a portion of the Arctic National Wildlife Reserve to oil and gas production; and he has reversed a ban on certain pesticides.

Trump's EPA, led by a former fossil fuel lobbyist, also re-opened fuel standards for passenger cars and trucks, including challenging California's right to set higher emission standards than the national standards in existence. In addition, he has dropped climate change as a national security threat and, instead, his administration is claiming increased domestic fossil fuel production is a national security benefit.

Fortunately, despite the president's efforts to undo the progress of the past few years, others, for the most part at the state level, recognize the scientific crisis we face. And they continue to seek measures to curtail carbon emissions, phase out coal and increase clean energy use, develop solar energy, use electric vehicles, and find alternatives to fossil fuels.

At some point, Trump will be an unpleasant, distant memory. The unanswered question is how much damage he will have caused the United States and the rest of the world environmentally during his tenure, and whether the efforts of Democrats, once they regain the power of the presidency and Senate, can reverse Trump's attempts to turn back the environmental clock.

DEREGULATION

We know what deregulation has done to the environment. At least those who believe in climate change know the damage deregulation has done environmentally.

Yet, there is much more to deregulation that environmental deregulation. Two other examples of the Trump era—education and banking deregulation.

Trump's education department has limited the scope and authority of higher education accreditors. Rather than having those accreditors determine which organizations should enforce federal student aid rules, the education department will now make those determinations. As part and parcel of these changes, the department's rules allow colleges to make changes without the approval of accrediting agencies.

Then, there is the Public Service Loan Forgiveness program of 2007, which was replaced by the Temporary Public Loan Forgiveness program of 2018 to help those who were having trouble meeting the terms of the 2007 program. If it sounds Orwellian, it is.

Meant to provide loan forgiveness to those who make monthly payments for a period of 10 years while engaged in broadly-defined public service, the program, managed by the Education Department, has not cured the problem. Why? Because the Education Department has rejected 99% of those who applied under the 2018 program.

In addition, following federal and state investigations into fraud at for-profit colleges that were shuttered, students suddenly found the bar for debt forgiveness raised by the Education Department. Incredibly, at colleges like Trump University (which was forced to shut its doors and to settle claims against it for $25 million), students were left with incomplete degrees, debt, and difficulty in having that debt forgiven.

While education deregulation is obviously problematic, it is banking deregulation that should concern all of us. During his presidential run, Trump promised to roll back the 2010 Dodd-Frank Wall Street Reform and Consumer Protection Act, a bill passed after the meltdown following the 2007-8 Great Recession.

Dodd-Frank recognized the import of several large banks to the economy (and, accordingly, the need to rescue them from collapse because they were too big to fail). But it also put in place rules that prevented banks from using customer deposits in risky bets, required banks to have specified capital reserves, and implemented stress tests to determine whether, in case of another financial crisis, a bank would remain solvent.

In 2018, Dodd-Frank was replaced by the Economic Growth, Regulatory Relief and Consumer Protection Act. Under the act's terms, smaller banks were let off the hook, with more stringent regulations applied to banks that had $250 million or more in assets. Small and midsize banks, whose failure would not threaten the US economy, would, therefore, save money on stress testing and be left with more funding for lending.

Importantly, the Volcker Rule (named after the former Federal Reserve Chairman) was also modified. Whereas in the past, banks were banned from engaging in proprietary trading (placing their own financial bets with money from customer deposits) and, instead, were to focus solely on trades for their clients, Trump's deregulation legislation permitted smaller banks (those with less than $10 billion in assets) to speculate.

Rather than providing strong capital requirements for all banks, smaller banks were exempt from those requirements. As a result, they were not required to hold back cash or other liquid assets to provide a cushion of assets should a financial crisis develop.

Dodd-Frank was instrumental in establishing strong capital requirements for banks, which were required to reserve a certain amount of cash or bonds to insure stability should the markets go into free fall. In the world of Trump and his acolytes, though, there appears to be no concern for the future, whether of the environment, education, or finance.

MINIMUM WAGE

The question of raising the minimum wage seems appropriate on a number of levels. First, the wage paid workers should keep up with inflation; second, a person making the minimum wage should be able to support a family without having to work multiple jobs; and third, the minimum wage should allow wage earners to lift their families out of poverty.

What seems obvious, however, is, in fact, not reality. For instance, minimum wage earners are often second-wage earners, who are simply supplementing the primary wage-earner's income. Or, maybe they are students, perhaps high school students, who are earning "spending money."

A higher minimum wage, which clearly has appeal to people who are employed at that level, may well run into the proverbial rule of unintended consequences, though. As wages go up, businesses have to decide whether they can continue to employ the existing workforce or whether they need to downsize or automate to reduce their costs.

Higher wages are, obviously, great for those who retain their positions. For those who are forced out of work, however, the higher wage is meaningless, and they are, unfortunately, "collateral damage."

Another unintended consequence: Jobs are reallocated from small businesses to larger operations. Simply stated, "mom-and-pop" businesses cannot afford to pay the higher wages because their margins cannot support those costs.

Finally, there is the obvious consequence—prices will go up for consumers. Who else, other than consumers, is going to bear the cost of increased wages?

Looking at these factors in the aggregate and citing statistics from the Congressional Budget Office, a $15 minimum wage established uniformly across the United States would increase the take-home pay of 17 million people and lift 1.3 million people out of poverty. However, there would also be a high cost: Between 1.3 and 3.7 million people would lose their jobs.

If the minimum wage is going to go up (as it already has in several areas), we need to recognize one size does not fit all. For example, why should someone working in rural counties be paid the same as a person working in an urban area? He or she shouldn't because the living costs for the rural worker are less than the costs of those employed in a city.

It seems the reasonable approach to an increase in the minimum wage would be to have it closely reflect the local or regional economy. Once established, though, the minimum wage should be indexed to inflation. In that way, people can be paid more fairly without running the risk of large numbers of others losing their jobs.

EQUAL PAY FOR WOMEN

It is hard to believe that, in 2019, we are still talking about whether women should receive equal pay for equal work. Obviously, they should.

We have come a long way when, in 1848, women gathered in Seneca Falls, New York to issue a Declaration of Sentiments, and when, 115 years later, John Kennedy signed the Equal Pay Act of 1963. Yet, more than five decades after Kennedy signed the Equal Pay Act, women are earning 79 cents for every dollar a man earns for doing the same work. (For women of color, the wage gap is even greater.)

Despite the fact it is illegal to pay men and women working in the same place differently for similar work, the disparity continues. It is in no one's best interests—not the employer, not the male employee, and certainly not the female worker—for the practice to continue.

If men and women are paid fairly (and equally) for equal work, morale at the workplace is enhanced. As morale increases, productivity grows. Everyone wins!

In addition, paying people equally for equal work negates the threat of costly legal actions. It also makes it easier to recruit and retain workers.

According to the World Economic Forum, which annually examines the gender pay gap, it will take decades to address the issue of parity across the globe. In the case of the United States, parity will be attained in 208 years at the rate we are now addressing the issue.

If a reason for the gender pay gap is to be singled out, motherhood is often cited. As women take the time to begin a family, a gap develops between the male and female worker, which is euphemistically labelled the "motherhood penalty."

Of course, there is an easy "fix" to the problem. During the past 50 years, there has been a 3000% increase in the growth of women-owned businesses. If any organization should be free of a gender pay gap, it would be a business started by a woman. Presumably, women working at those businesses would not face a "motherhood penalty."

Aside from working at a woman-owned business, women should hope for all employers to do the right thing. And the right thing is to pay men and women equally for equal work.

ABOUT THE AUTHOR

A lawyer by training, Roger Hull was a corporate attorney, counsel to the Governor of Virginia, a member of the National Security Council task force on law of the sea, and a college president for 24 years at Beloit and Union. Author of several books, including one on the Vietnam conflict (which he co-authored) and another on the conflict in Ireland, Hull is the founder/president of a foundation whose dual objectives are to change the lives of at-risk children through the creation of after-school programs on college campuses and to provide construction training for unemployed / underemployed adults.

Made in the
USA
Middletown, DE